'Snow White'
Music and lyrics by Colin Magee. Script by Andrew Oxspring

***IMPORTANT

Dear Customer,

Here is your copy of **'Snow White'** by Colin Magee and Andrew Oxspring. We trust it will provide you with everything you need to put on a memorable production.

Please read carefully the **Performance Licence Application** details on page 2 of this booklet. For any performance of drama, narrative and dialogue from published materials like this you are legally required to purchase a valid performance licence *from the publishers* – in this case Edgy Productions. This is standard practice. Please note that *local authority issued licences, PRS and CCLI licences do not cover these performances.*

If it is your intention to only use this material within the classroom as a learning activity, or to just sing the songs only in assemblies (using overhead transparencies) and not to an audience of parents, no fee is due.* In these circumstances you are covered by those licences mentioned above. *If, however you intend to make photocopies for any of these purposes, a fee is payable.*

Please photocopy then complete the form on page 2, and post us your performance details (with fee if applicable) no later than 28 days before your first performance, and a licence will be issued.

Should you have any questions regarding this matter, or the staging of **'Snow White'**, please get in touch and we will be happy to help in any way we can.

* Where no fee is due you are still obliged to return a Performance Application form – see page 2

'Snow White'
Music and lyrics by Colin Magee. Script by Andrew Oxspring and Colin Magee

***************** **IMPORTANT** *****************

PERFORMANCE LICENCE APPLICATION FORM

For **any** performance of **SNOW WHITE**, a valid performance licence from Edgy Productions **must** be held. Please note, **your PRS, MCPS or CCLI licence does not cover you for performances of this production**. Please ensure you complete and return the relevant sections of this form, along with the fee where applicable, at least 28 days before your first performance. You can also apply online at www.edgyproductions.com For performances where an admission charge is made, a form will be sent which you should return with 10% of the takings (plus VAT @ 17.5%) within 28 days of the final performance.

By ticking please indicate which performance licence applies to you, and send a photocopy of this form along with the fee (where applicable) to:

Permissions, Edgy Productions, 4 Queen Street, Uppingham, Rutland LE15 9QR

A copy of your Performance Licence will be posted to you

Licence 1	Licence 2	Licence 3
For up to 5 performances in one year, of only the songs, within school, to only staff and children of that school, at which no admission is charged, and for which no rehearsal photocopies are made:	For up to 5 performances in one year, of the script and/or songs, to the public/parents, at which no admission is charged:	For up to 5 performances in one year, of the script and/or songs, to the public/parents, at which an admission charge **is** made:
NO FEE ☐	**£25** *(inc VAT)* ☐	**£25** *(inc VAT)* + 10% of takings *(plus VAT @ 17.5%)* ☐
This licence allows only the use of handwritten transparencies of songs. No photocopies allowed	This licence includes permission to photocopy the script and songs	This licence includes permission to photocopy the script and songs

Composers /script writers rely on payments from public performances for their livelihoods. Please ensure they receive their dues

NAME..........................SCHOOL..

ADDRESS...

TEL............................. EMAIL...

Number of performances.......... Dates of performances from .... to ....

I enclose a cheque for £25 *(if applicable)* payable to Edgy Productions Ltd ☐

'Snow White'
Music and lyrics by Colin Magee. Script by Andrew Oxspring and Colin Magee

INTRODUCTION

It's a story that never seems to stop thrilling children. The traditional tale of 'Snow White' has everything they could wish for – action, adventure, magical characters, suspense, tension, gruesome bits, soppy bits, lots of laughs and a 'happy ever after' ending. Perfect! This production keeps all those ingredients, and with a couple of 'Edgy' extras thrown in for good measure it's a great recipe for a thoroughly entertaining show.

Eight up-beat and catchy songs complement a clever and hilarious script, which brings to life all the well known, and a few not so well known characters. With some subtle modern twists, but not forsaking any of the classic storyline, this musical will engage every audience of parents, teachers and children.

Amongst others, we find ourselves in the presence of a wicked shopaholic queen, a Snow White whose vocation is to teach animals literacy and numeracy, seven vertically-challenged forest dwellers with various obsessions for food and cleanliness, evil boffin inventors, fawning cronies with a clever spin on the magic mirror…... and many more! There's plenty of scope for good old-fashioned character acting, with parts that children will relish getting stuck into and really hamming up!

With narrators keeping things moving, the well-paced script tells the whole tale from 'Once upon a time…' to wedding bells. Every song is adaptable so your whole cast can be involved in each singalong chorus, and with solos available anyone who wants to shine will get the opportunity.

So, good luck with the show – we're sure it will be a riotous success!

'Snow White'
Music and lyrics by Colin Magee. Script by Andrew Oxspring and Colin Magee

CHARACTERS
(Individual speaking parts in order of appearance)

4 Narrators   Our fairy tale-tellers

The Good Queen   'Broody' is an understatement

3 Courtiers   Ensuring palace affairs run smoothly

The King   Not overly-blessed in the brains department

The Bad Queen   Scheming shopaholic

Her 3 Cronies   Fawning underlings

Snow White   Banished beauty whose refuge is reading, 'riting and 'rithmetic

2 Animals   Quite literally the teacher's pets

The Woodcutter   For the 'chop' if he can't control his conscience

Chief   The not-so-big boss ⎤

Beamer   Pint-sized smiler

Milton   Diminutive disinfectant

Muncher   Petite pie-addict ⎬ **The Teeny Tribe**

Snuffles   Knee-high nasalist

Grouchy   Miniature moaner

Snoozy   Over-tired titch ⎦

3 Evil Boffins   Crocodile clips put smiles on their lips

The Prince   Devastatingly dashing

2 Hunters   Tally-ho whip-crackers

(Ensemble characters)

Courtiers	**The Bad Queen's Entourage**
Woodland Animals	**The Prince's Entourage**
Evil Boffins	**Wedding Guests**

'Snow White'
Music and lyrics by Colin Magee. Script by Andrew Oxspring and Colin Magee

Scene 1

*(To **intro music** the lights come up. The scene is a palace, represented by 'his' and 'her' thrones. Four narrators stand to one side. The Good Queen sits alone, knitting.)*

Narrator 1 ~ Once upon a time in a far-away land
Stood an old Palace, majestic and grand.
Here lived a Queen, so gentle and kind,
And a King with his brain in his fat behind!

Narrator 2 ~ Nevertheless all their subjects were loyal,
And palace life could be described as 'right royal'.
But one thing was missing from their regal home -
A child who would one day inherit the throne.

Good Queen ~ Alas, I cannot pretend I am happy,
I yearn to be changing my first dirty nappy.

Narrator 3 ~ And as the queen sat by her bedroom window,
Mournfully knitting one more baby-grow,
Her finger was pricked and the blood trickled down,
Staining the snow outside on the ground.

Good Queen ~ All that I wish for, if the truth be told,
Is my very own baby daughter to hold.
Lips red as roses, a cute button nose,
And a heart that's as pure as the clean driven snows.

Narrator 4 ~ Now, they say in the old days, whenever snow fell,
Old Mother Nature was casting a spell.
The royal courtyard became quite enchanted,
As if by magic the Queen's wish was granted.

*(To the **baby gurgling** sound effect a 'bundle' is thrown on, and caught by the Queen.)*

Narrator 4 ~ So settle yourselves, take the weight off your pins.
'Cause folks, this is where our story begins!

(Enter rest of the cast for the opening song.)

Song **Here Comes The Show** - see page 18
(Whole cast)

(All exit, leaving three of the king's courtier's chatting to one another. There is a 'vacant' sign placed on the Queen's throne.)

Narrator 1 ~ Now things in the palace were really amiss,
A case of real awfulness, such a crisis!

Courtier 1 ~ I'm not one for gossip……..

Narrator 1 ~ The courtier lied……..

Courtier 1 ~ But I hear on the grapevine the Good Queen has died!

'Snow White'
Music and lyrics by Colin Magee. Script by Andrew Oxspring and Colin Magee

Courtier 2 ~ We know. It's a tragic and terrible thing,
But shhh, keep a lid on it, here comes the king.
His tiny mind can't handle such dreadful news,
So we told him she went out shopping for shoes!

(The King enters, carrying the baby, pacing around and clearly worried.)

King ~ Well this is just great! We've an absent 'first lady',
While muggins here is left holding the baby.
Oh where is the woman? I've phoned all the shops,
But no-one's laid eyes on her. Let's call the cops!

Courtier 1 ~ Not the police, Highness, don't be a berk.
They're all snowed under with paperwork!

Courtier 3 ~ She'll turn up, your Majesty, just wait and see.
There's really no reason for you to worry.
I suggest, in the meantime, you tend to your daughter.
You could both play with the doll's house you bought her!

(The King exits with the baby.)

Courtier 2 ~ The poor chap's that brainless, in a month or so
He'll forget about her! He need never know!

Courtier 3 ~ But someday he'll need someone new on the scene.
Let's find candidates for the post of 'New Queen'.

(The courtiers exit.)

Narrator 2 ~ Accept our apologies for butting in,
But with tales like these when time's running thin,
We need to push on, we're feeling the squeeze,
So, sound effects person, fast-forward please.

*(To the **time fast forward** sound effect all courtiers enter with the King, who is blindfolded, as if to be presented with a marvellous surprise.)*

Narrator 3 ~ Cue the gold-digger in search of fortune,
Full of hot air like a....well....hot air balloon.
Nose to the ceiling, she struts and she swaggers,
Barking her orders, her eyes shooting daggers.

(Enter the Bad Queen with her entourage of fawning cronies. The courtiers remove the King's blindfold, and he looks in disbelief, then cowers behind them.)

Courtiers ~ Your Majesty, we are so proud to present
Your wife. Don't you agree she's 'heaven-sent'?

(The look on the King's face tells us he definitely doesn't agree!)

Song <u>Out With The Old, In With The New</u> - see page 19
(Sung by the Bad Queen, her cronies and the whole cast)

'Snow White'
Music and lyrics by Colin Magee. Script by Andrew Oxspring and Colin Magee

Bad Queen ~   Now away with you all, I have money to spend.
The boutiques are open, there are balls to attend.

(Everyone but the Queen exits. Three of her cronies then return with an object covered with a sheet.)

Narrator 4 ~   Then once the Queen checked all the riff-raff had gone,
She ordered her magical mirror brought on.

(One crony lifts the sheet, under which is an ornamentally framed picture of a glamorous woman. The Queen sits on her throne. As the second crony fusses over the Queen, touching up her hair, the other two give the picture a quick seeing to with a feather duster. When ready they indicate to the first crony to let the Queen look. All three cronies then stand behind the picture, using it to hide from the Queen.)

With her best Victoria Beckham pout
This mountain of make-up, this silly old trout
Smiled at the mirror and huskily called….

Bad Queen ~   Who, in this land, is the fairest, of all?

Narrator 1 ~   Let's wait before hearing the mirror's reply
As there is a detail we must clarify.
The Queen's cronies, sick of this twice-daily farce,
Had years ago taken out all of the glass!

Crony 1 ~
(from behind the frame)   Instead, it's a picture of a catwalk model,
And 'cause she's so vain, tricking her is a doddle!

Crony 2 ~
(from behind the frame)   She thinks that it speaks and tells her the truth,
So desperate is she to recapture her youth.

Crony 3 ~
(from behind the frame)   And even though she's got the face of a horse,
It's us three who tell her……..

All Cronies ~
(in disguised voices)   Why, you are of course!

Bad Queen ~   That's right! And if anyone should disagree
It's…*(she draws a finger across her neck making a garrotting sound)*
Right. Shopping. Come on, follow me.

*(To the **dramatic music** the cackling Queen flashes her oversized gold credit card, and they all exit. The lights fade, the thrones are removed, and cut-outs of trees are placed around to represent a forest.)*

Scene 2

*(Snow White skips on as the **forest music** plays. She is followed by the frolicking woodland animals. They all dance for the duration of the music. As it fades the animals sit in a semi-circle, with Snow White at the centre sitting on a log or tree-stump, engaging them in conversation.)*

Narrator 2 ~   Permit us again to skip forward in time, *(Time **fast forward** sound effect)*
But now we are a few years down the line.
Things at the palace went from bad to worse,
As if it were under a sinister curse.

'Snow White'
Music and lyrics by Colin Magee. Script by Andrew Oxspring and Colin Magee

Narrator 3 ~ Since her dramatic arrival at court
The Queen ruined everyone's life, as she brought
Unhappiness, fear and mistrust in her wake.

All ~ Can't someone sort her out for goodness' sake?

Narrator 4 ~ Now, do you remember the King had a child?
A beautiful girl, with a nature as mild
As an angel. She had not a single bad bone,
(pointing at audience) Unlike the little monsters you have at home!

Narrator 1 ~ To Snow White the Queen took an instant dislike,
And short of asking for her head on a spike
She'd banished the girl to a forest one night.
Here Snow White grew up, out of mind, out of sight.

Snow White ~ Sent from my kingdom like some common thief.
My stepmother's cruelty just beggars belief.
I miss my dear father, my childhood friends too....

All Animals ~ Now we're her chums! Yes it's strange, but it's true!

Animal 1 ~ She meets us here, 9 o'clock, each single day.
She teaches us science and maths, how to play
Chess and backgammon. She speaks French a bit,
Works hard for charity but won't mention it.

Animal 2 ~ A more perfect person you never could meet,
And having her here is an absolute treat!

Song It Will Be Alright, Snow White - see page 20
(Sung by Snow White and the Woodland Creatures, supported by the whole cast)

(As the music ends, the Queen's three Cronies enter side-stage)

Narrator 2 ~ But who else was skulking among the dark trees?
None other than the Queen's evil cronies.

Crony 1 ~ My! Who's that beauty with such striking features,
Hanging around with the four-legged creatures?

Crony 2 ~ A more gorgeous specimen I've never seen!

Crony 3 ~ Get a grip, Romeo! We must tell the queen!

*(To **dramatic music** the cronies exit in one direction, Snow White and the creatures in another. The lights fade, the trees are cleared and the thrones are brought on.)*

Scene 3
(Back at the Palace the Bad Queen's entourage enters, followed by the King and the Queen herself, who is leafing through a catalogue whilst nagging the King. The King and Queen sit on their thrones, and the other characters take positions around them.)

Bad Queen ~ And then there's this ball-gown with matching shoes…
Mmm….beige or brown ones? It's so hard to choose.

'Snow White'
Music and lyrics by Colin Magee. Script by Andrew Oxspring and Colin Magee

King ~ You'll have me broke before the month is out!
No more shoes. (*Aside*) Oh no, here comes the pout.

Narrator 3 ~ She complained that beauty didn't come cheap.
He took his bank statement, to read it and weep!

(The King exits, studying the bank statement, grumbling to himself. The Bad Queen gestures orders to her cronies.)

Narrator 4 ~ Now the Queen really did need cheering up.
She asked for her mirror and bag of make-up.

Crony 1 ~ Bring her Majesty the magic mirror!
(aside) And also the trowel and the polyfiller.

(Cronies 2 and 3 fetch a huge collection of beauty products, and the framed picture. The Queen slaps on some lipstick and face powder then pouts at the picture.)

Bad Queen ~ Mirror, oh mirror, you beauty expert,
Who in this land is the best bit of skirt?

(There is a silent pause. Crouching behind the picture the cronies have their hands over their mouths, eyes screwed up tight.)

Come on, come on. I haven't all day.
Who is most beautiful? Hurry, just say.

Narrator 1 ~ The cronies were fit to burst, eyes screwed up tight.
They blurted their answer out………

Cronies ~ Ma'am, it's Snow White!

(There is stunned silence as the Queen descends into a rage.)

Bad Queen ~ WHAT DID YOU SAY TO ME, YOU PIECE OF JUNK?

Narrator 2 ~ It's fair to say the atmosphere now stunk!
The cronies repeated the name of Snow White,
The girl the Queen had banished one fateful night.

Bad Queen ~ AAAAH! ORDER THE WOODCUTTER TO SEAL HER FATE,
TO BRING ME HER STILL-BEATING HEART ON A PLATE!

*(To **dramatic music** all exit. The lights fade, the thrones are removed and the trees brought back on. Snow White and the animals enter. The animals sit in rows, facing the front, holding exercise books.)*

<u>Scene 4</u>

Narrator 3 ~ The animals loved spending time with Snow White,
But the smell in the air told them all was not right.

(The Woodcutter enters with an axe. The animals protectively gather round her.)

Woodcutter ~ Don't be afraid, there is nothing to fear.
I'm just a gentle woodcutter, my dear.

'Snow White'
Music and lyrics by Colin Magee. Script by Andrew Oxspring and Colin Magee

> I promise you that I'm not up to no good,
> I'm just here doing my job – chopping wood.

(The animals move back into their rows, facing the front, their heads in their books. Snow White moves among them checking their work. She stops by an animal on the back row, the woodcutter behind her.)

Narrator 4 ~ And so they continued with Latin translation,
Worksheets on adverbs, long multiplication.
On algebra, map-reading, physics they worked,
So unaware of the danger that lurked!

(The woodcutter picks his moment, and raises his axe to strike Snow White from behind. She, and all the animals, turn around and gasp. The woodcutter freezes, then drops his axe and falls to his knees.)

Narrator 1 ~ When push came to shove he just couldn't do it
Chopping up ladies was wrong, and he knew it!

Woodcutter ~ Run, Snow White, run, and never come back.
Your life is in danger, you're under attack.
The Queen wants you wiped off the face of the earth.
Run Snow White, run for all that you're worth.

Snow White ~ Oh thank you, woodcutter, for sparing me so.
Deeper into the dark forest I'll go.
Farewell my furry chums, you've been great buddies,
Please don't forget to keep up with your studies.

(She runs off. The woodcutter stands and shakes his head.)

Woodcutter ~ I'm too kind-hearted. Will I never learn?
I'm for the chop if I fail to return
Without a heart. What on earth can I do…….?

(He pauses, then spying the animals a grin spreads over his face.)

Look, little creatures, I've something for you.

*(The woodcutter extends his hand as if tempting the animals with a treat. They sniff and cautiously approach. When they get close enough the woodcutter raises his axe, the animals squeal and, to the **chasing music,** dart off in different directions. As the lights fade the woodcutter chases the animals on and off the stage/around the room. Before the music ends seven sleeping bags, a small table laid for dinner and seven chairs are brought on stage. Some, but not all of the trees have been removed.)*

Scene 5

(The scene is The Dwarves' house. There is a knock on the door. Snow White enters.)

Snow White ~ Hello, hello. I don't mean to intrude,
But could you please spare me a morsel of food?

Narrator 2 ~ The seven small sleeping bags, seven small chairs,
The seven small knives and forks laid out in pairs,
The seven small portions of food made it clear
That seven small people had set up home here.

'Snow White'
Music and lyrics by Colin Magee. Script by Andrew Oxspring and Colin Magee

Snow White ~ I've never stolen, for stealing's a crime.
But I'm starving, so maybe just this one time.

Narrator 3 ~ So she took a little from every plate,
And despite her feelings of guilt, she ate.
Then, quite remorseful, poor Snow White she wept,
Dried her eyes, said her prayers, curled up and slept.

*(Snow White lies down on a sleeping bag. To her **snoring** the seven dwarves enter.)*

Song **The Teeny Tribe** - see page 21
(Sung by the Seven Dwarves, supported by the whole cast)

Chief ~ Oh life is so joyous, to live it a pleasure.
An honest day's work, with the evenings for leisure.

Beamer ~ Comedy shows on the late night telly,
A few cool beers and some food in my belly.

Milton ~ Right, we must wash our hands, or germs will spread

Muncher ~ Please, can't I first have just one slice of bread?

Snuffles ~ Achoo! Hey! Hang on, I sense something weird.

Beamer ~ Don't worry Snuffles, it's only your beard!

Milton ~ You should keep it trimmed and dust-free. Serves you right!

Grouchy ~ Bah! Someone's left on the living room light.

Snoozy ~ That's not all, Grouchy. My legs feel like lead,
But I can't go to sleep 'cause someone's in my bed!

(They gather round Snow White. Chief shakes her arm and she awakes, startled.)

Snow White ~ Oh please, little person, let go of my arm.
I promise sincerely I mean you no harm.
For days I've been running, afraid and alone.
Exhausted, I came across your lovely home.

Snuffles ~ Achoo! So you say that you've been on the run?
Why is that? Tell us, girl. What have you done?

Narrator 4 ~ She opened her heart to them, she spilled the beans.
Her story of palaces, banishment, queens,
Animals, forests and woodcutters too,
Had them in tears by the time she was through.

Snow White ~ Take pity on me. Oh, please let me stay.
I'll cook and I'll iron and clear things away.
I'll teach you lessons in lots of subjects,
And help you improve your career prospects.

(The dwarves huddle together to discuss the matter. Snow White looks on hopefully.)

Beamer ~ I'm happy to tell you the answer is yes!

'Snow White'
Music and lyrics by Colin Magee. Script by Andrew Oxspring and Colin Magee

Milton ~ If you promise to care for us? Tidy our mess? *(She nods eagerly)*

Chief ~ Okay, then it's sorted. You're welcome Snow White.
But let's go to bed now, it's been a long night.
Grouchy looks teed off, and Snoozy is yawning,
Your tenancy contract can wait until morning.

*(To the **intro music** the lights fade and everyone exits. The furniture and trees are removed and the thrones are brought back on.)*

Scene 6

Narrator 1 ~ We mustn't allow concentration to lapse,
So let us, good audience, fill in some gaps.
Back at the palace things had moved on,
The Bad Queen assumed that Snow White had now gone.

Narrator 2 ~ She'd asked of her mirror the question of old,
And in no uncertain terms she had been told
That Snow White still lived, as gorgeous as ever.
News that did more than just ruffle a feather.

(The Bad Queen enters with cronies. She carries a tray from which she takes mouthfuls of 'food'.)

Bad Queen ~ That wretched woodcutter betrayed me, the swine.
He's had his comeuppance. Vengeance is mine.
He's paid the price for what he has done.
Anyone fancy some woodcutter tongue?

(She offers the tray to the cronies who look disgusted, and try not to be sick!)

Crony 1 ~ There's only one option, as far as I see,
To get back to some sort of normality,
To sort out the problems which still torment us,

Cronies ~ It's time to bring out the boffin inventors!

(The Boffins enter, carrying tables on which elaborate scientific equipment is set up.)

Song **The Evil Boffins** - see page 22
(Sung by the Evil Boffins, supported by the whole cast)

Crony 2 ~ The things you've come up with had better impress
What have you got?

Boffin 1 ~ Well, this tight fitting dress!
A poisoned comb, a poisoned apple too.
Evil inventions, Majesty, for you.

(Boffin 1 presents the Queen with the three items. She looks at them, unimpressed, and hands them to the cronies, who follow her off.)

Boffin 2 ~ It's the best we could do in so little time.
If they don't work, that's our necks on the line!

'Snow White'
Music and lyrics by Colin Magee. Script by Andrew Oxspring and Colin Magee

Boffin 3 ~ Well, if they're duds it's the end for us boffins.
I bet she's already polishing our coffins!

(The boffins exit, nervously packing up and removing their equipment and the thrones. The lights fade.)

Narrator 3 ~ I'm sorry, the action is dragging again.
At this rate we won't be finished 'til ten!

(to the sound effects person) Be a sport, hit the 'fast forward' once more.... *(time fast forward sound effect)*
Thanks for that, and for the two times before!

Narrator 4 ~ Now, the Queen found Snow White's cosy new home,
And tricked her into using the comb.
The poison worked, but on the brink of death,
As the poor girl took her final breath,
The seven dwarves rushed in to save the day!
They revived Snow White and chased the Queen away.

Narrator 1 ~ Soon after that the Bad Queen returned.
You'd think that Snow White by now would have learned,
To spot the signs, to heed the dangers
And never to open the door to strangers.

Narrator 2 ~ Disguised, the Bad Queen persuaded Snow White
To put on the dress, which she tied up real tight.
But as Snow White lay gasping for air,
To her attacker's utter despair,
Our heroes arrived and saw off the Queen,
And that brings us up to date. Ok, next scene.

*(To the **intro music** the dwarves' furniture and a few trees are brought back on. Snow White is dusting while the dwarves get ready to go to work.)*

Scene 7

Chief ~ Goodbye Snow White. Now you mind what we said.
Don't open the door or you may wind up dead!

Narrator 3 ~ So they left for work, Grouchy grumbling,
Milton fussing, Muncher's tummy rumbling,
Snoozy yawning, Snuffles sniffling,
Chief and Beamer happily whistling.

(The Dwarves exit. Snow White starts to sweep the house)

Snow White ~ How kind of the chaps to increase my chores,
Concerned I was getting a little bit bored.
They're also letting me work for free,
Said I'd be insulted receiving money!

Song Life is Wonderful - see page 23
(Sung by Snow White, supported by the whole cast.)

(Before the last bars of the song there is a knock at the door and the mood of the music changes. Snow White answers when the song is finished.)

'Snow White'
Music and lyrics by Colin Magee. Script by Andrew Oxspring and Colin Magee

Snow White ~ Who's there…?

Narrator 4 ~ …..asked Snow White, feeling quite tense.

Bad Queen ~ A frail old pedlar, selling sticks of incense.
(off-stage) I've fruit from the orchard, a real tasty treat,
Ripe plums and pears…….and apples so sweet.

Snow White ~ I'm sorry, I really can't open the door.
So just go away and visit no more.

Bad Queen ~ But surely you're hungry. I'll ask you again,
Please let me in, my dear…

Snow White ~ Oh, go on then!

(The Bad Queen enters, dressed as an old pedlar)

Narrator 1 ~ So Snow White let this harmless old crone
Through the front door and into her home.
And it doesn't take a genius to guess
Just what the silly young girl did next!

(In slow motion the Queen hands Snow White the apple. She takes a bite, clutches her throat and falls dramatically to the floor. The Queen bends down to check her pulse. Happy that Snow White is dead she punches the air, then clicks her fingers. Her cronies enter carrying the mirror.)

Bad Queen ~ Ok, mirror, now surely this time
The prettiest face in the kingdom is mine?

Cronies ~ Spot on, your Majesty! Yes, it's quite true
(from behind the frame) Nobody here is more gorgeous than you.

*(To **dramatic music** the Queen and her cronies exit, cackling, leaving Snow White lying on the ground. The Dwarves return home after a hard day's work.)*

Chief ~ After a hard day's work I'm so looking
Forward to feasting on Snow White's home cooking.

Beamer ~ Will it be salad?

Grouchy ~ No! Something hot!

Muncher ~ I really don't care, I just hope there's a lot!

(Half asleep, Snoozy doesn't notice Snow White on the floor, and trips over her.)

Snoozy ~ What the….? Hey everyone, look down here!

Milton ~ What? Is there dust she's forgotten to clear?
If you want a job doing then………………

Chief ~ Hush, Milton, please.

Narrator 2 ~ Each of the little guys sank to his knees,
And stared at Snow White lying lifeless and still.
She'd taken a step beyond being just ill!

'Snow White'
Music and lyrics by Colin Magee. Script by Andrew Oxspring and Colin Magee

Grouchy ~ Bah! It is no use. I just cannot save her.
It must have been something the Evil Queen gave her.

Snuffles ~ Snow White, come back to us. Please be pretending.
Sniff! I can't face such an unhappy ending.

Chief ~ I'm so sorry fellas, she's headed for heaven.
Eight minus one – we're back to just seven.

Narrator 3 ~ And stricken with grief they lifted Snow White,
And carried her body out into the night,
To bury her in the woods she loved so,
Amongst all the furry friends she'd come to know.

*(The lights fade and to the **funeral music** four dwarves carry Snow White off stage, while the other three clear the furniture, and bring on the rest of the trees.)*

Scene 8

*(As the funeral music continues the Dwarves enter carrying Snow White, followed by the animals. They lay her on the ground and all gather round her in mourning. As the music comes to an end we hear the sound of **hunting horns** at which the animals cower in fright. The prince and his entourage enter.)*

Prince ~ Tally Ho! This way chaps! Follow that deer!
(noticing the crowd) Whoa! Hold your horses! What's going on here?

Hunter 1 ~ It seems like a meeting has been organised,
On your land, Highness! I'll have them chastised.

Grouchy ~ Your presence here, gentlemen, is desecration!
You're hunting a large part of our congregation!

Snuffles ~ Isn't it obvious we're all in mourning?
How dare you intrude on our grief without warning.

Hunter 2 ~ Allow me, oh Highness, to deal with this chap.
He shouldn't be talking to royalty like that!
I'll flog the scoundrel with my riding whip,
For being so bold as to give you such lip!

Prince ~ No! Stay your hand and leave them all be.
Hurt anyone and you'll answer to me.
Forgive us good fellows, and animals too,
For bursting in like this and disturbing you.
But please be so good as to tell me why
You're all gathered here, so watery of eye.

Chief ~ Our faithful new friend, full of love and trust,
Has departed this life – she's bitten the dust.
We've come to this place which she loved the best,
To say farewell and lay her body to rest.

(The Prince and Hunters gather round Snow White's body, astonished at her beauty.)

'Snow White'
Music and lyrics by Colin Magee. Script by Andrew Oxspring and Colin Magee

Hunter 1 ~   Her beauty's enough to make any man weep.
Even in death she looks only asleep.

Prince ~   For years I have been looking for someone like this.
I can't help myself, I must give her a kiss!

Hunter 2 ~   Don't do it, your Highness! Just think for a minute.
This match has no future. Best not to begin it.
She's dead as a dodo. Of breath there's a lack!

Prince ~   Exactly. A missus who can't answer back!
I'm joking of course! Yes, I know that you're right.
It's just that I've never beheld such a sight.
It's tragic our love is denied a beginning…..

Hunter 3 ~   Oh no! Here we go! He's gonna start singing!

Song **Here All Along** - see page 24
(Sung by the Prince and Snow White, supported by the whole cast)

Prince ~   Stone the crows! You're back from the dead!
Tell me, my love, was it something I said?
Was it the stirring speech that I gave?

Snow White ~   No, it's the whiff of your cheap aftershave!
It smells reminds me of an old billy goat!
The fumes have dislodged what was stuck in my throat.

Chief ~   Whatever the reason, Snow White, you're alive!

Beamer ~   My grinning has gone into overdrive!

Snoozy ~   Such wide-awake feelings 'til now I've not known.

Snuffles ~   Achoo! But she's right 'bout his Eau de Cologne!

Grouchy ~   Even I've got a sensation of glee!

Muncher ~   Snow White, does this mean you'll be cooking our tea?

Milton ~   Oh yes, and the toilet is due a good bleaching!

Animal ~   And there's more French vocab that we need teaching!

Prince ~   I'm sorry folks, but she'll be coming with me,
Back to my palace, and we shall marry.
Assuming you're up for it, Snow White, my dear?

Snow White ~   Hmmm…. *(sizing him up)* Yes, you'll do! Let's get out of here!

*(To **intro music** all exit cheering. The trees are removed and new thrones brought on.)*

Scene 9

*(The lights come up and the whole cast enters. The bad queen, cronies and deceased characters can be now dressed as courtiers. As **wedding trumpets** sound Snow White and the prince walk through the cheering crowd, and sit on two new thrones.)*

Courtier ~ My Queen, there's an old fellow at the gate,
Says he's your father, and sorry he's late.

(To more cheers the old King comes forward. He and Snow White tearfully embrace.)

Narrator 4 ~ On seeing each other again their hearts leapt,
They shattered the hugging world record, and wept.

Narrator 1 ~ The king told his daughter the saddest of tales,
Of how their domestic life went off the rails.

King ~ After she got her feet under our table
That hag slipped me potions 'til I was unable
To do more than sit there and dribble, while she
Fleeced me dry on one giant shopping spree!
A steaming great cart full of lies she then told,
That wild beasts took you when you were five years old.
And zonked to the eyeballs I believed what she said,
And thought, all these years, that my Snow White was dead.

Snow White ~ Oh Father, dear Father, it matters not now.
You're here with us all, but I'd like to know how
You escaped from her clutches to find me again.

Narrator 2 ~ They all gathered round to hear him explain.
On learning that Snow White survived her last hit
The dastardly Queen had thrown such a fit.
Her boffins, afraid of the temper she'd shown,
Had turned her into a garden gnome.

King ~
(spoken slowly to the audience)
Now she sits on the lawn unable to move,
And dogs cock their legs against her! Goes to prove
You shouldn't be nasty! Be lovely instead,
Or unpleasant things will rain down on your head!

Narrator 3 ~ So everyone's joyful, they're all on cloud nine,
But I'm sorry, we've come to the end of the line.
So with songs in our hearts, with glasses held high,
With this happy ending we bid you……

All ~ GOODBYE!

Song *Everything's Turned Out Fine* - see page 25
(Whole cast)

THE END

'Snow White'
Music and lyrics by Colin Magee. Script by Andrew Oxspring and Colin Magee

Here Comes The Show
(Whole cast)

1. Hello and welcome to our little rendezvous.
   We're glad to have you come along.
   Clap hands and make some noise 'cause
   We are the girls and boys who
   Have all the music and the songs

   If it's fun that you're after, excitement and laughter,
   For a jam-packed hour or so
   Then just kick of your shoes
   And if you happen to be snoozing
   Wake up, here comes the show!

2. Our mighty meaty fairytale
   Concerns the story of a girl.
   Come on we've got it all in
   Some handy sized instalments.
   Just step into our wacky world.

   There's a clot for a husband who's hopelessly accustomed
   To the life of Old Riley.
   There's kindness and malice,
   Where the vertically challenged
   Are real pleasures to meet.

3. But there's a sorry sadness to it all,
   For not everyone survives to smile through it all.
   For our tale is like both life and football…
   Some you win and some you lose.

'Snow White'
Music and lyrics by Colin Magee. Script by Andrew Oxspring and Colin Magee

Out With The Old, In With the New
(The Bad Queen, her cronies and the whole cast)

All ~   Yes she's the Queen,
Her beauty is so great that it's obscene,
With talents deeper than the deepest sea,

Cronies ~   And we won't disagree 'cause she's the queen

Queen ~   They wouldn't dare,
'Cause I can kill a puppy dog with just one stare.
These idiots just wouldn't have a prayer.

Cronies ~   And we don't say a word because were scared.

All ~   Out with the old, in with the new,
Things are gonna change, though we don't want them to!

Queen ~   Everything's going to be dandy and fine,
With my gold credit card and too much spare time.

               I'm so adored,
But being so admired can be a chore.
Look at the countless magazines my face adorns.

All ~   More like the mug that sunk a thousand ships and more!

Cronies ~   Oh its no laugh
Working for a full on psychopath.
If she was any more stuck up she'd be a giraffe,
But we can't say a thing, were only staff.

All ~   Out with the old, in with the new
Things are gonna change, though we don't want them to!

Queen ~   Everything's going to be dandy and fine,
With my gold credit card and too much spare time.

'Snow White'
Music and lyrics by Colin Magee. Script by Andrew Oxspring and Colin Magee

It Will Be Alright, Snow White

(Snow White and the Whole cast)

All ~ Life in the city is bustling and busy,
But here in the woods we're a world apart.
The sound of birds singing, the little stream murmuring,
A paradise sure to melt hardest of hearts.

Snow White ~ But at night when the moon and stars dance in the sky
I lay my head down to sleep,
Dream of castles and loved ones so far, far away,
And wake with a tear in my eye.

All ~ It will be alright, Snow White. Alright Snow White.

How someone could do her wrong we'll never understand,
Whilst she is in our hands she'll come to no harm.
Wherever, whenever she leaves us forever
'Til then we'll just cherish each moment we have.

But at night when the moon and stars dance in the sky
She lays her head down to sleep,
Dreams of castles and loved ones so far, far away,
And wakes with a tear in her eye.

It will be alright, Snow White. Alright Snow White.

'Snow White'
Music and lyrics by Colin Magee. Script by Andrew Oxspring and Colin Magee

The Teeny Tribe
(The Seven Dwarves and whole cast)

All ~ The teeny tribe,
AKA Magnificent Seven.
They're pocket sized
Always in their beds by eleven.
Famously,
The daring dwarves, or mighty miracles,
If you please.

Dwarves ~ So full of trust,
Always proud with heads in the clouds.
Rely on us
To get things done on time or thereabouts.
So let us now
Introduce the rest of our crew,
If you please…….

1 2 3 4

Chief
Milton
Muncher
Grouchy
Snuffles
Beamer
Snoozy

The teeny tribe,
Dressed in leather *or* **Birds of a feather** *(if not wearing leather)*
All rent together
'Cause we cant afford to buy.

'Snow White'
Music and lyrics by Colin Magee. Script by Andrew Oxspring and Colin Magee

The Evil Boffins
(The Evil Boffins and whole cast)

All ~ They're the Evil Boffins,
Boffing is their game.
Making crude inventions,
Some say they're insane.
Crazy!

Boffins ~ When we were at school we
Didn't act too socially.
While everyone played rounders
We had Bunsen burners.
We don't mind whom we work for,
As long as we are free
To really excel, brew funny smells,
Making the most of our brain cells.
Overpaid and qualified,
We will rule the world!

All ~ Haven't time for girlfriends,
Boyfriends make them flee.
Yes they prefer explosions
And electricity!
'Cause they're the Evil Boffins,
Boffing is their game.
Computer chips, crocodile clips
These put a smile upon their lips.
They like taking notes in their lovely white coats,

Boffins ~ And we will rule the world.

(instrumental during which the boffins 'play' with the equipment)

We're the Evil Boffins,
Boffing is our game.
Making crude inventions,
Some say we're insane.
All ~ Crazy!

'Snow White'
Music and lyrics by Colin Magee. Script by Andrew Oxspring and Colin Magee

Life is Wonderful
(Snow White supported by whole cast)

Snow White ~   Lucky me!
I had the world upon my shoulders,
But look at me now.
Oh wow!
And goodness me!
Things will be oh so fine,
Now that we've become friends.
Look around,
What a happy place!

All ~   Thank the lord!
Oh when you feel so good
You want to sing a song.
Sing along.

And gracious me!
Oh when you feel that
Nothing ever could go wrong,
Something's always bound to go wrong………………

(before the song ends we hear the Bad Queen rap on the door)

'Snow White'
Music and lyrics by Colin Magee. Script by Andrew Oxspring and Colin Magee

Here All Along

(The Prince supported by whole cast. During the song Snow White wakes up and joins in!)

Prince ~   Here, as you lie in my arms so still,
I can swear that I've never
Felt like this before and don't think ever will again.
Oh, what I'd give for just one small kiss.
For it seems like a crime that
Somebody so sweet should have to fade away like this

All ~   He rode far over mountain plain,
Sailed the oceans but all in vain.
Just when he felt like giving in
He finds you here…
And you were here all along

(Snow White stirs, and wakes up. To everyone's surprise she stands and sings!)

Snow White ~   My, who is this holding me so tight?
From the strength in his arms he might
Be everything I need
To bring me back to life.

All ~   He'd ride far over mountain plain,
Sail the oceans and through the rain,
Swears he'll never look again
Now he's found you.
And you've been here all along.

'Snow White'
Music and lyrics by Colin Magee. Script by Andrew Oxspring and Colin Magee

Everything's Turned Out Fine
(Whole cast)

1. We're sad to say that time has come,
   We've almost reached the end,
   So to the sound of wedding bells
   We wish you well, good friends.

   And in the end everything's turned out fine,
   Just like you hoped it would.
   'Cause after every storm the sun will shine,
   Just like you knew it could.

2. All journeys have their twists and turns,
   We don't know what's to come,
   So next time you feel sad or lost
   Just keep in mind this song.

   And in the end everything's turned out fine,
   Just like you hoped it would.
   'Cause after every storm the sun will shine,
   Just like you knew it could.

   And in the end everything's turned out fine,
   Just like you hoped it would.
   'Cause after every storm the sun will shine.
   Just like you knew it could.

'Snow White'
Music and lyrics by Colin Magee. Script by Andrew Oxspring and Colin Magee

STAGING AND PRODUCTION SUGGESTIONS

The action in 'Snow White' alternates between a palace, a forest and the dwarves' house. With minimal scenery, changing between the three will be easy, and only requires a simple stage layout.

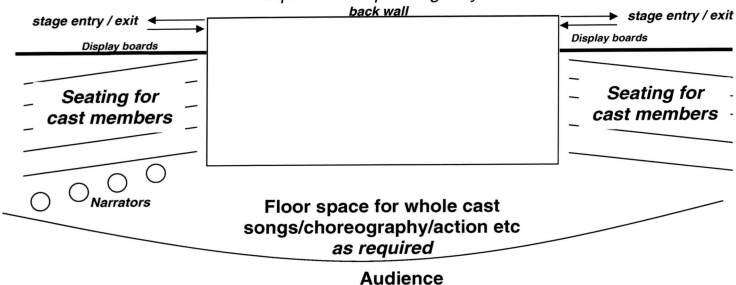

- **Scenery** – A large backdrop or picture on the wall behind the stage could depict a fairytale scene of a clear blue sky, a palace on a hill, with rolling forests below. This will cover all bases for imagining the individual scene settings. A large coat of arms could be displayed and removed to add to the feel of being in a regal setting for when the palace scenes take place, whilst small cut-out trees and bushes can be placed round the stage for the forest scenes. Alternatively, if you have the resources, three separate and interchangeable backdrops showing more detailed views of the palace, forest and dwarves' home would look very professional.

- **Furniture** – Two high backed chairs can be covered and decorated with red and gold finery to represent thrones. Infants' chairs and table, with toy tea sets would be perfect for the dwarves' home, and seven sleeping bags will eliminate the need to find or make beds.

- **Props** – For the mirror, find/buy a poster of a glamorous woman, perhaps a model or popstar, and attach it to a decorated wooden frame. The evil queen will need a large handbag for her beauty products and gold credit card, and later a tray of 'nibbles' and an apple. The good queen needs knitting needles and a baby doll, the king a sceptre perhaps, and the wood-cutter a pretend axe. The forest animals should carry text and exercise books, and Snow White a briefcase perhaps. The dwarves could enter and exit the house carrying spades, forks buckets etc. The boffins will need measuring cylinders, tubes, batteries, wires etc secured to a table that can easily be carried on and off. The prince and hunters could carry whips and horns.

- **Use of Space** – The whole cast will probably want to be involved in the performance of all the songs. A space on the floor in front of the main stage could be used to accommodate extra bodies. In this space, for some songs, the cast could perform dance routines.
  A seating area for resting performers could be allocated either side of the stage. This lets them enjoy the performance as part of the audience, allows easy movement on and off the stage, and of course eliminates the need for back-stage supervision.

- **Costume** – You may want to stick with the traditional fairytale costumes associated with Snow White – lots of pairs of tights, cloaks, gowns etc. Alternatively you could mix old and modern styles. The king (who should still have a crown) and male courtiers could wear suits, female courtiers also. The good Queen could wear something 'pretty' in stark contrast to the bad Queen who could wear vulgar, clashing items in fur and leopard skin, with a boa and ridiculous heels etc, covered with simply a shawl for when she visits the dwarves' house as a pedlar. Snow White should perhaps remain quite traditional, in a white dress. The boffins could wear lab coats and protective goggles and have soot marks on their faces. A traditional look may suit the dwarves, with lederhosen as the song suggests, and floppy hats and smocks. They could, however, wear hard hats and overalls to depict their work. Either way their individual characteristics should be identified - a beard for Snuffles, marigolds for Milton, a MacDonalds bag for Muncher etc. An idea would be to have their names on their tops. The Prince and hunters could be in red jackets and jodhpurs or something befitting their 'country' status.

- **Content** – Feel free to adapt the script and storyline if and when you feel it's appropriate. You can include additional songs or pieces of music for choreography if you want to lengthen the production, or cut sections if you require a shorter show. Make it your own.

- **Audience seating** – Finally, we suggest the audience be seated at tables (cabaret style), and encouraged to bring drinks and nibbles of their choice. If this is being performed as an end of year or leavers' show, a relaxed party atmosphere will really make the evening go with a swing, and give parents, staff and children something to remember for a long time. Please email, phone or write to us if you have any production queries at all, and we'll be more than happy to help.

Above all enjoy your rehearsals and performances – they should be a lot of fun!

'Snow White'
Music and lyrics by Colin Magee. Script by Andrew Oxspring and Colin Magee

'Snow White'
Music and lyrics by Colin Magee. Script by Andrew Oxspring and Colin Magee

2. Out With The Old, In With The New

(The Bad Queen, her cronies and the whole cast)

'Snow White'
Music and lyrics by Colin Magee. Script by Andrew Oxspring and Colin Magee

'Snow White'
Music and lyrics by Colin Magee. Script by Andrew Oxspring and Colin Magee

3. It Will Be Alright, Snow White

(Snow White and the whole cast)

Piano Arrangement by Peter Merry   Music and Lyrics by Colin Magee

© ℗ Edgy Productions 2005. Unauthorised performing and copying prohibited. See p2

Verse 2 How someone could do her wrong we'll never understand,
Whilst she is in our hands she'll come to no harm.
Wherever, whenever she leaves us forever
'Til then we'll just cherish each moment we have.
But at night when the moon and stars dance in the sky
She lays her head down to sleep,
Dreams of castles and loved ones so far, far away,
And wakes with a tear in her eye.

'Snow White'
Music and lyrics by Colin Magee. Script by Andrew Oxspring and Colin Magee

5. The Evil Boffins

(The Seven Dwarves and the whole cast)

'Snow White'
Music and lyrics by Colin Magee. Script by Andrew Oxspring and Colin Magee

6. Life Is Wonderful

(The Evil Boffins and the whole cast)

Piano Arrangement by Peter MerryMusic and Lyrics by Colin Magee

© ℗ Edgy Productions 2005. Unauthorised performing and copying prohibited. See p2

Verse 2   Thank the lord!
Oh when you feel so good
You want to sing a song.
Sing along.

And gracious me!
Oh when you feel that
Nothing ever could go wrong,
Something's always bound to go wrong……………

'Snow White'
Music and lyrics by Colin Magee. Script by Andrew Oxspring and Colin Magee

7. Here All Along

(The Prince supported by the whole cast)

Piano Arrangement by Peter Merry

Music and Lyrics by Colin Magee

Lyrics:

Here, as you lie in my arms so still. I can swear that I've never felt like this before, and don't think ever will again. Oh, what I'd give for just one small kiss. For it seems like a crime that somebody so sweet should have to fade away like this.

All: He rode far over mountain plain, Sailed the ocean but all in vain. Just when he felt like giving in

'Snow White'
Music and lyrics by Colin Magee. Script by Andrew Oxspring and Colin Magee

'Snow White'
Music and lyrics by Colin Magee. Script by Andrew Oxspring and Colin Magee

8. Everything's Turned Out Fine
(Whole cast)

Piano Arrangement by Peter Merry

Music and Lyrics by Colin Magee

© ℗Edgy Productions 2005. Unauthorised performing and copying prohibited. See p2

'Snow White'
Music and lyrics by Colin Magee. Script by Andrew Oxspring and Colin Magee

'Snow White'
Music and lyrics by Colin Magee. Script by Andrew Oxspring and Colin Magee

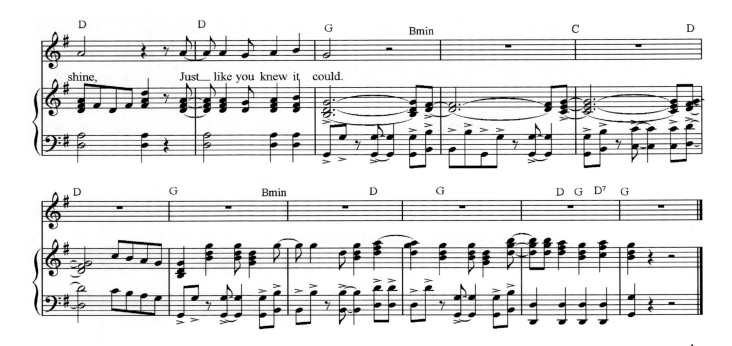

Verse 2 All journeys have their twists and turns,
We don't know what's to come,
So next time you feel sad or lost
Just keep in mind this song.

And in the end everything's turned out fine,
Just like you hoped it would.
'Cause after every storm the sun will shine,
Just like you knew it could.